You Can't BUY LOVE... But You Can RESCUE IT

Heartfelt Stories on Pet Adoption

KPT PUBLISHING

photography by:
{julie johnson}

You Can't BUY LOVE... *But You Can* RESCUE IT

Copyright © 2018 Photography by Julie Johnson, Vine Images Inc.

Published by KPT Publishing
Minneapolis, Minnesota 55406
www.KPTPublishing.com

ISBN 978-1-944833-34-3

Design and production by Koechel Peterson and Associates, Minneapolis, Minnesota

First printing December 2018

10 9 8 7 6 5 4 3 2 1

Printed in the United States of America

INTRODUCTION

It's time to…stop. Listen. Smell the flowers and feel the breeze. There is no rush. Enjoy this moment. These are just some of the lessons we learn from our rescue dogs.

It's said that joy is the simplest form of gratitude. Joy is what rescued dogs experience and share! Dogs are inherently kind souls, and when we can learn to live life like *a dog,* we have learned one of life's great lessons about the meaning of unconditional love.

Gene Hill was right when he said, *"Whoever said you can't buy happiness forgot little puppies."* But had he read this book first, he would have added another sentence to it: *"You can't buy love…but you can rescue it."*

S oon after we married, my husband and I decided to adopt a rescue dog. Our search ended quickly when we saw this gorgeous shepherd with Wheaten Terrier mix on a rescue website. She looked perfect! We couldn't make an appointment fast enough. The report said Penny was about eight months old, had been abandoned, had no aggression, was acceptable for children and loving—she sounded perfect! We decided that day we couldn't leave her, and she joined our family.

When we got her home, we wondered if the report was for another dog. Penny had major food aggression, was terrified of cages, and was very leery of certain men. Someone had mistreated her. One day I tried to add food to her bowl while she was eating, and she snapped at me, then she growled and cornered me in the kitchen as though she was going to attack. My husband came home to find me on the kitchen counter, crying in fear, with Penny still barking fiercely at me. I was thinking, *Can we keep her? Will she be safe with children?* But my husband never wavered. Penny was a part of our family, and we wouldn't give up on her. We just had to find the right person to help us.

We found a local trainer who has an amazing ability with rescue dogs. She worked for the next year on Penny's fears and anxieties, and finally she became more trusting of us. We got rid of the kennel so she was never locked up, and that helped her be more comfortable at home. Her fear of certain men still exists, but overall she is more secure.

Three years ago, we welcomed our daughter, Locklyn, into the world. Penny immediately loved her, although she didn't like being woken during the night! And Penny loved having me home all day on maternity leave. As Locklyn could do more, the two of them began to interact with each other, and now they're best buddies! Locklyn considers Penny her big sister. All those fears of food aggression related to a child were for nothing. In fact, Penny will even share her food with Locklyn, although we've stopped that when she tries. And Penny loves that Locklyn is at the perfect height for kisses on the face!

Penny brings us all so much joy every day. We couldn't imagine our life together without her. We now have a second baby on the way, and I know that Penny will love our new little one as much as she loves Locklyn. I see the three of them growing up as siblings and getting into a lot of mischief!

Whenever I imagine what Penny's favorite story might be, I see her lying in a bed, under the blankets, saying, "Please tell me the story of how you rescued me again."

A Word from Penny

Give lots of kisses every day.
Real kisses are big and wet
and sloppy and say
"I love you" without a word.

My boyfriend, Daniel, had Kody as a delightful little puppy during a previous relationship. Due to unfortunate circumstances related to their breakup, she took Kody with her despite all the training and the incredible bond he and Daniel shared. Days went by, then weeks, then months, and then years, with Daniel not knowing where Kody ended up or whether he was even still alive. The only information he received had come soon after the breakup, with her saying that she had given Kody away. That cut Daniel straight to the heart.

Daniel so loved and agonized over the loss of Kody that for ten years he kept Kody's puppy collar and picture beside the bed. Ten years. I remember how often he would pick up the collar, run his fingers along the edge, and stare at the photo, saying, "I really wish I knew where my best friend was."

Fast-forward to three years ago, and we were looking for a rescue dog to add to our family. We searched one rescue site after another. Then we clicked on one site's "Available Dogs," and to our utter shock there was a photo of a dog that looked just like Kody staring

at us! His picture and the description matched perfectly to Daniel's description. *We had found Kody!* Full-throated screams and shouts followed! We immediately called the humane society and said to put him on hold because we are on our way to adopt him. We raced to get there, and sure enough, Kody knew who Daniel was immediately, tail wagging! You can only imagine our elation and the tears of joy that flowed.

The people at the humane society were nearly as shocked as we were. They said that Kody had been bounced from home to home and gone through abusive owners. He had been in and out of the shelter many times, and he had extreme trust issues due to his past. They actually had to keep Kody in a corner all by himself because he had become so unfriendly.

Regardless of the circumstances and how much Kody had changed, we were taking him home no matter what! Having heard Kody's story, the humane society dropped all the adoption fees, and we were on our way to give Kody a new start and a forever home. A decade after Daniel lost his best friend, he had him back!

Three years later, and we're still somewhat in disbelief that we have Kody. Of course, Kody is the most amazing dog in the entire world! It took some time to rebuild his trust, but every second has been well worth it! He is our best friend and family member. It may have taken us all those years to find him, but we never gave up.

A Word from Kody

The best day in my world is a day spent with the ones I love. My richest memories start and stop with them.

Sydney, my first rescue dog, has shown me how to face life's struggles and suffering and yet come out the other side full of love, trust, and happiness. This sweet apricot toy poodle was found wandering the streets, severely malnourished with matted hair covered in fleas. The pound estimated Sydney to be fourteen years old and took her straight to a rescue due to her health condition. I absolutely adore poodles, and when I first saw her, my heart broke and a sudden burst of indignation filled me. Sydney was so weak she could barely walk, and her head drooped forward, as though she was about to crumble in a heap. Every one of her teeth was abscessed.

I spent the first few days hand-feeding Sydney , hoping she would gain strength. She was so anemic that I took her to see an internal medicine specialist, who deemed her a case of neglect. Fearing cancer as the cause of her severe anemia, she underwent a bone marrow biopsy. She also required a full dental extraction.

The good news is that she recovered from the anemia. Furthermore, once she regained her health, Sydney was estimated to be around four years old! She now loves to run and play outside, to chase frogs, and oh how she loves to eat.

Despite everything Sydney went through in her recovery, I felt with a certainty that she wanted to live. Through all her various tests, she never complained. She only loved. She only had kisses and snuggles for everyone involved in her care.

Nora is my other delightful toy poodle. After she was rescued, it took her many months to recover from physical and emotional abuse. When I adopted Nora, she was far less trusting than Sydney and had no interest in humans or food. She was severely underweight, had swollen, fearful eyes, and began vomiting. Through various scopes and diagnostics, it was determined that Nora has an autoimmune condition causing her stomach issues. She also needed a full dental extraction and suffered a broken jaw due to infection. You would have never guessed she was in any pain at all—she is so stoic!

Once Nora began to feel better, she flourished. Although she is a senior dog, she started to run and play again. It is such

a thrill to watch the transformation of an innocent animal from having borne years of silent pain and suffering to being free of the pain and fear right before your eyes. Nothing can be more rewarding.

These two lovely girls teach me so much about myself, my priorities, and what really matters in life. Caring for medical and palliative care dogs can be emotionally and physically draining, such a rollercoaster! Seeing how happy these two goofballs are makes it worth it all!

I would love to tell you about our lovely old lady named Jellybean. She is an eleven-year-old pit bull that is a true advocate for her muscular, bully breed. She is caring and lovable, demands attention, showers you in kisses and affection, and is as stubborn as she is strong. She also possesses the superpower of being able to hear a bag of chips open two houses down the block.

I have been involved with and passionate about rescues for many years. I was roaming aimlessly on Facebook when one of the rescues where I volunteer had a slew of senior dog postings. I had just found my most recent foster dog an adopted home and was ready for something a little more permanent for our household. What I really wanted was to give a senior dog a home to live out its days.

I read a posting that stopped me in my tracks. Jellybean had been dumped at the rescue with a cancerous tumor. The tumor was successfully removed, and she is a cancer survivor! I had to see Jelly, so I made the arrangements to meet her, and it just seemed as though it was meant to be when I arrived. Even her rescue felt as such. That day she came home with me to stay!

Jellybean has changed our lives in ways we wouldn't have ever thought possible. We already had one pretty amazing American Bulldog named Beefy Chunks. He's younger, but the two of them act as if they've been friends for years. And Jelly is good with my young children, letting them drape blankets over her and lead her around the house like their prized pony, or allowing them to use her body as a bridge so the tractor can cross the water.

I never expected the comfort that Jelly has given me. The past year brought nothing but bad health issues for me, as I was diagnosed with not one, but two autoimmune diseases before my thirtieth birthday. It's been a tough year. The days are tough. But at the end of every long day, Jellybean

refuses to take no for an answer when it comes time to cuddle at night. My husband works nights, so I'm often alone, which can make depression worse. She makes it known that I'm not alone by simply resting her big old head on my butt in bed. She's been nothing if not another family member to us.

I'm so glad I found her. I can tell you I love this dog deeply. She fills my heart to the brim.

A Word from Jellybean

Just come alongside and stay by their side. Without saying a word, your presence says, "We'll get through this together."

I have always loved the bully breeds, so with that in mind I spent countless hours searching *all* the dog rescues within a two-hour drive from my home. Finally, after being deeply disappointed by not finding the right fit, I was ready to give up when a rescue shelter offered to break protocol and take me into the back so I could see all their dogs. I walked down rows of kennels, but none of the dogs caught my eye. Then I suddenly saw him, an American Bulldog cowering in the back of his kennel, and my heart swelled. As I approached, he charged, jumping at the chain-link fence and snarling at me. Most people would be terrified of a ferocious bulldog packing one hundred pounds of muscle, but I saw a dog begging me for help, even though I didn't understand it. Everything about him looked wrong, but something about him just seemed right.

I asked if I could take him out, and once he was outside, he lost his aggressiveness, though he dragged me wherever he wanted to go. I was told that two years previous he'd been surrendered by a couple who had never trained him and said he was out of control. Always overlooked, he sat in shelters unwanted

for two full years until the day I found him. He seemed crazy, and I was just crazy enough that I adopted him on the spot.

I soon realized how much work Blue would require. He snapped at strangers and was extremely reactive with other dogs and cats, so I enlisted dog trainers to help. Several trainers quit within the first few months, saying he was a lost cause. Friends told me to take him back, but something about Blue stopped me from giving up. I sensed that he was willing to learn, but, being a true bulldog, he was stubborn and needed someone to match his stubbornness. I took that challenge and spent hours every day working with him. Over time, he slowly changed from an unpredictable dog to a gentle, affectionate dog with exceptional manners.

Like many other rescue dogs, Blue did not come as the perfect pet. I gave him a home, but more importantly I gave him the second chance no one else was willing to give him. He needed a lot of love, and he wanted to please, but nobody had ever asked anything from

him. When he challenged someone, they backed away and gave up. I was the first person willing to put in the time and persevere, to push back, work with him, and teach him. He went from being a dog that reacted in fear to a confident dog that doesn't need to react.

Blue taught me to never give up, and I discovered a sweet dog with a heart of gold that always has my back…all because I took a chance on him!

A Word from Blue

Never judge a book, a dog, or a person by their looks. What matters is what's on the inside.

COCO

The moment sweet little Coco arrived at the rescue shelter where I worked, I knew he was "ours." I grew up with Dachshunds and had recently lost my own fifteen-year-old male. We only knew that his name was Coco and that some foreign exchange students had kept him during their time in school but left him at the shelter just before returning to their home country. Once at the shelter, Coco was totally confused and didn't seem to understand a word of English. He also had some digestive issues, which I thought might be due to the stress of suddenly being alone at the shelter. I couldn't wait to bring our spunky boy home, and he fit right in.

What I didn't know was just how perfect the adoption timing was. You see, I had been an emergency veterinary technician as well as a shelter worker, which meant I was helping with animals that had often been subjected to great trauma and extreme abuse. Over time, their suffering got to me, and I had started to suffer from what is called "compassion fatigue."

I went through a period of major depression and was almost hospitalized. But our Coco, now called "Coco Bongo," knew that something was not right with his new momma, and he was determined to keep me from falling into what many famous writers have called, "That dark night of the soul." He stayed glued to my side every second of every dark, sad day, kissing my tears away. I don't know what I would have done if it were not for my faithful sidekick to help cheer me along and snuggle me away from my heartbreaking sadness. But he did.

Not long after I was emotionally healed we had another devastating issue to deal with. As it turned out, Coco's digestive issues were actually due to a large

mass in his abdomen. My husband and I decided to move forward with a very expensive surgery because as my husband said, "It's the least we can do to thank 'our boy' for his help in making you well." Thankfully, after they removed most of his bowel and the mass came back benign, our Bongo boy is healthier than ever and now runs and plays so much more than he ever did!

I truly believe I would not be here today had Coco Bongo not come into my life when he did. Surely, in all the world, there is no other dog so comforting and amazing. What I wouldn't do for my little wiener man!

A Word from Coco Bongo

Everyone gets sad from time to time. Heal human hearts by sitting close by, being silent, and nuzzling gently.

People ask me why I chose a rescue dog, but I tell them that Luna found me. I was volunteering as a screener with a dog rescue organization at the time. There was a miniature schnauzer mix that was arriving from Mexico, and they were looking for a foster home to take Luna in. Because of the timing, none of the regular foster homes were available, so I said I could keep her for the rest of that week. The report on Luna stated that she had been found roaming the streets of Cozumel and not surprisingly was dog aggressive, on various medications, and healing from a variety of ailments. Caring for her temporarily didn't seem like a big deal.

Before I met Luna, I had been interested in another rescue dog, but over the next four days that all changed. How could I resist the charm of her walrus moustache, her bushy beard and eyebrows, and her personality that's three times as big as she is. And her soulful eyes that followed my every movement, and her quivering excitement to go outside for a walk. She made me laugh every day. Needless to say, little Luna crept onto my lap and into my heart, and I made the decision to adopt her.

Some rescue dogs have behavioral issues that result from their prior experiences, and Luna is no exception. Luna's dog aggression stems from her experiences with her owners or as a street dog, so I've been working with dog trainers to identify corrective and positive reinforcement methods to adjust her behavior and make her life a lot less anxiety driven. She's been able to become friends with my parents' dog, and he is teaching her that being around dogs can be a positive experience.

A Word from Luna

If you express your love,
it will be returned.
If you ask for love,
you'll get love.
Be bold. Be irresistible.

Luna loves people of all ages, and she's introduced me to a lot of my neighbors (and their dogs). In so many ways she's recalibrated the focus of my life. As a single woman living alone, my focus had been on my daily life, whereas now my focus is Luna, her well-being, her training, and her growth as a dog. We explore neighborhood trails, travel together, hang out together, and she's enabled me to grow as a human being as well and to better interact with the people in my life.

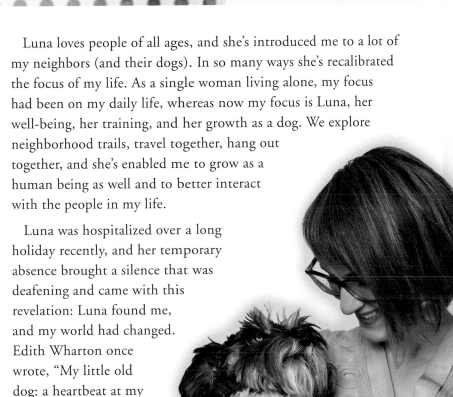

Luna was hospitalized over a long holiday recently, and her temporary absence brought a silence that was deafening and came with this revelation: Luna found me, and my world had changed. Edith Wharton once wrote, "My little old dog: a heartbeat at my feet." I can say that's true for me of my little Luna.

Some years ago I started fostering rescue dogs. Living alone in a downtown condo and working a nine-to-five job kept my involvement temporary, as most dogs need a yard and lots of attention. However, once I met Roxy, a Jindo mix that I call Foxy Roxy, all bets were off. Roxy had lived in a wire bottom crate in a South Korean shelter since she was born. No one wanted her, so for the first two years of her life that is literally *all* she knew. They were about to euthanize her when she was rescued, and she came straight from the airport to my place to be fostered.

Imagine what is what like for Roxy to finally discover a life outside of a cage. She was so sweet and gentle and quiet and curious, but she was so overwhelmingly fearful. Everything was new and frightening—wind, cars, leaves, bikes, grass, open spaces, noises, and anything moving—everything except her crate. When she was overwhelmed, she'd just sit. Sometimes she'd sit on a walk and just watch the cars go by. She loved sitting with her eyes closed with the wind blowing gently in her face and parting her hair as it blew. I'll never forget the first time she ran...she scared herself! And it took her a long time to

gain spatial awareness, she was always hitting things.

What I didn't understand is that Jindos usually bond with their first owner, and she was growing to trust me. I didn't notice it happening because, with her being so fearful, she'd be in her crate most of the day and not explore. I'm used to dogs that need constant attention, and this little girl was so independent and happy to be on her own. Well, about one month in she was starting to build her confidence and slowly started to explore my apartment. Then she started getting playful. She has a beautiful smile! I've never had a dog that smiles like her! I couldn't give her up. We're a good little pair. I decided to adopt her.

Seeing her grow and come out of her shell (well, her crate) makes me so happy. I can't believe this neglected little girl is so confident now! We can actually walk around a city block and she does just fine. And when she's in a new place and gets scared, she comes to me. When she snuggles, she just melts right into me. She loves other dogs and just sits and licks their noses. Seeing her start to play still fills me with joy and butterflies, and I just put everything down and watch her.

I cannot imagine life without my Foxy Roxy! It's been amazing to watch her explore, and learn, and become brave. She's a happy girl now, and so am I!

A Word from Roxy

The world is a fascinating place, and everyone you meet is interesting, and no two people smell the same. Smile a lot and share your pleasures.

I have always had a soft spot for rescue animals. When we lost our family cat, Mikey, whom we had rescued as a senior, we felt as though a piece of our family was missing. Our daughter was especially brokenhearted. So I started to search for a rescue dog this time, but for some reason none of the dogs I was seeing felt right. A couple of months after I began to look, I came across a post about rescues coming from Shanghai, China. Curious to learn more, I clicked on the post, and there was the most adorable terrier named Roger. Something shouted yes inside, and I fell instantly in love with him! I contacted the woman who shared the post, and she helped change our lives and Roger's forever. Within a month, Roger arrived to our delight.

I kept in touch with the woman who helped me get Roger, and she said that he had bonded with another dog named Bean. They had both been living at a construction site and were badly malnourished. She told me that prior to their rescue, little Bean and Roger were both on their way to being euthenized (dog meat is a delicacy in China).

Once I had been filled in on the details and saw photos of Bean's dark piercing eyes, my heart melted over the amount of suffering that we could relieve. Before long Bean was on a plane and on her way to a whole new life. When she arrived, she was terrified and clinging to life. Her skin was infested with parasites. I immediately took her to the vet, who gave her frequent antibiotic injections and medication for the parasites. Little by little she has improved and is so very sweet!

About a month later, I contacted my rescue friend again and stumbled upon an itsy-bitsy Chinese dog named Molly. She was a street dog trying to survive in a very cold, cruel and terrible place. I was overwhelmed by the haunting look in her eyes, and thought that Bean and Roger were just the medicine she needed to help her recover. I can only

imagine the stories she would tell me if she could talk. I guess her eyes told me enough.

These three lovely rescue dogs escaped an abominable fate and have changed our lives in so many wonderful, intangible ways that I can't describe in words, but have enriched our lives with very tangible happiness. My daughter's heart has healed from the loss of her cat, and we have three new babies to love and spoil! And we are!

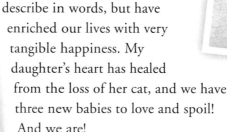

A Word from Bean, Roger, and Molly

Through life's ups and downs, attitude is everything. Where you start is not important. Where you finish is what matters.

TOBY

Twelve years ago marks the rescue of Toby, our fourteen-year-old miniature poodle, which forever changed our lives. Her mentally unstable owner tried to set her on fire, and the police and fire crew at the scene were able to save her. One officer called my mother, who worked for a rescue organization, and she quickly took Toby to the vet and began looking for a foster home.

Well, long story short, we are foster failures! We took Toby in temporarily, but we could never ever give this little bundle of joy away. We never thought we would take a dog, but once we got to know her, she won us over! The sad story attached to her and those dark oval-shaped eyes and wide, close-hanging ears were our undoing. But perhaps it was her initial fear of everything that soon turned into an undying love and adoration of our family members that made Toby a perfect fit for us.

Toby quickly got our family into a healthy routine of two or three long walks a day, getting up early to let her "out," feeding times, and then of course belly rubs! Anything but a "sissy," as some people think, in her younger years she was like a miniature athlete, moving

with a light, springy gait and dashing moves. In her golden years we've noticed even more how she pays rapt attention to each of us and quickly picks up our moods and behavior. There's nothing she loves more than being surrounded by us.

Not long ago, our fishing boat capsized and we almost lost Toby. She got trapped under the boat in frigid water. My husband, by the grace of God, was able to pull her out, and we rushed her to an emergency vet clinic. The vet on call told us that most people would euthanize their dog at that point, but for us that wasn't an option. Unfortunately, that led us to another vet whom we later learned was charged with cruelty to animals. No wonder Toby shook and trembled every time we took her there! She knew.

Fortunately, though, our new vet did X-rays on Toby and said that she was not only suffering from secondary drowning but was in congenital heart failure. Our previous vet never even told us she had a heart condition that with treatment perhaps could have prevented this. Our new hero vet prescribed just the right medications…and here we are, Toby is still with us. He calls her his "miracle dog," and my administrator has asked what life Toby is on!

Toby has taught us to be more compassionate and loving, showing us what unconditional love, devotion, trust, and loyalty mean. We will keep Toby loved, comfortable, and happy up until her last moments. We are forever grateful to have had her in our lives.

A Word from Toby

Love unconditionally…
without any expectations.
Teach others the meaning
of devotion.
Live life to the fullest.

Chester is a ten-year-old Labrador Retriever mix that we adopted from a rescue organization several years ago. Apparently his owner had died, so he was taken to a time-limited shelter, which means the shelter has a time limit, and it euthanizes adoptable dogs to make space for newly incoming dogs. The term *adoptable* can be twisted to fit many interpretations. Even though there is nothing wrong with a dog, some people may consider that dog *unadoptable* simply because it has been on the adoption floor for several months and passed over by potential adopters. If he had not been rescued, our Chester would have been euthanized.

At the time our youngest son was really struggling with anxiety in first grade. My husband, who had long wanted a dog of his own, convinced me that having a dog in the house would be a great stress reliever. I somewhat reluctantly acquiesced, but only to an older dog, as I didn't want to go through puppy training. My husband started looking up rescues, and my nephew's wife, who is a dog trainer, helped us narrow down our list.

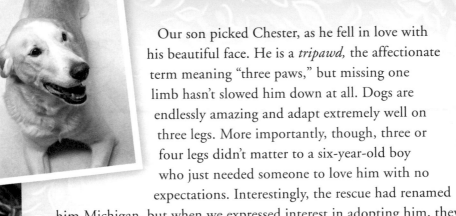

Our son picked Chester, as he fell in love with his beautiful face. He is a *tripawd,* the affectionate term meaning "three paws," but missing one limb hasn't slowed him down at all. Dogs are endlessly amazing and adapt extremely well on three legs. More importantly, though, three or four legs didn't matter to a six-year-old boy who just needed someone to love him with no expectations. Interestingly, the rescue had renamed him Michigan, but when we expressed interest in adopting him, they stated that his actual name was Chester. At the same time, *Chester* was the name of our son's favorite picture book, so it just seemed meant to be. You can imagine our son reading *Chester,* a story about an egomaniacal cat, to his new best friend, Chester the dog.

A Word from Chester

Be that friend who stays closer than a brother. Listen with your heart and talk with your eyes.

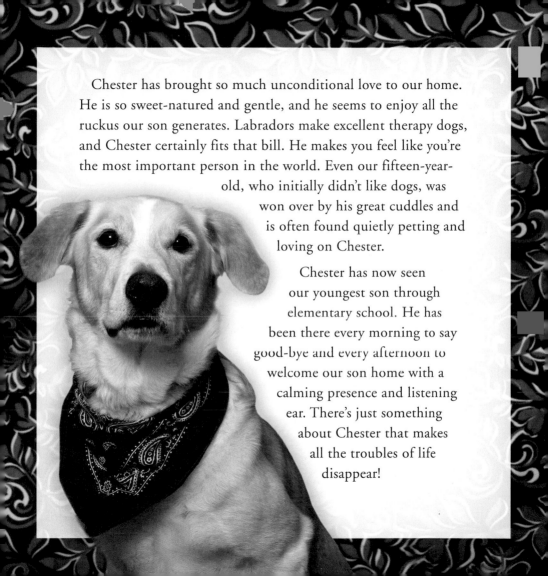

Chester has brought so much unconditional love to our home. He is so sweet-natured and gentle, and he seems to enjoy all the ruckus our son generates. Labradors make excellent therapy dogs, and Chester certainly fits that bill. He makes you feel like you're the most important person in the world. Even our fifteen-year-old, who initially didn't like dogs, was won over by his great cuddles and is often found quietly petting and loving on Chester.

Chester has now seen our youngest son through elementary school. He has been there every morning to say good-bye and every afternoon to welcome our son home with a calming presence and listening ear. There's just something about Chester that makes all the troubles of life disappear!

With three wonderful, energetic children, we wanted to find a mature rescue dog that needed a loving family who would provide companionship, instill a sense of responsibility in the children, and help teach them to be loving. We read up on King Charles Cavaliers and thought that a dog that is very dependent upon human companionship and that shouldn't be left alone too long couldn't go wrong in our house. We contacted a local rescue agency dedicated to finding homes for displaced Cavaliers.

We adopted Tucker last year when he was five years old, and our home has never been quite the same. As with all sweet-tempered dogs, there is potential to be timid, and he was very shy when he first came home with us. It's been wonderful to watch him bond with us and to see him come out of his shell. He fell in love with the kids immediately, and they with him. Tucker adores comfort, is always looking for hugs, loves snuggling on soft pillows, and never misses a chance for a good cuddle and a belly rub on one of our many laps.

Tucker is more athletic and outdoorsy than you might think, loving to entertain the kids by chasing birds and squirrels on their walks.

When he's not throwing his toys around the house and making the kids chase him, he's doing something with the hope that it will involve food, and preferably treats. Watching them have fun together always brings a smile to my face. Having a Cavalier means the kids are never alone in the house. I get surprised every once in a while when I see one of the kids and there's no little shadow nearby.

I've often thought that Tucker is more charming than any dog has a right to be, and he's just the right size too—not too big and not too small. I love how he's always interested to see what the kids are going to do next and more than willing to go anywhere and try anything. We can trust him to guard our house, but we've learned to never trust him to guard an unattended sandwich.

Tucker has been a perfect fit for our family. He senses when one of the kids is not well, and he delights to lie with them and shower some affection on them when they're home sick. Tucker has brought so much joy to our lives, and he will always be a part of our family. We are so blessed to have him in our lives!

A Word from Tucker

It's the little things
that matter in life.
If you can't find joy
in a stick or a lap
to snuggle in,
you're missing
the best parts.

Both my mother and I are huge animal lovers. My mother has a heart of gold and is a foster parent for a dog rescue. She has five dogs, three of which are hers, and two are most likely long-term or permanent foster dogs. They are so sweet, and each has an incredible rescue story.

Cupid is a Pyrenees mix that was born with no front legs and half a tail. Someone had abandoned him in a garbage can when he was a little puppy. He was rescued and placed with my mom to foster him. She eventually succumbed to his adorable puppy charms and welcomed him into her home permanently. Cupid is a constant source of daily entertainment as well as a great challenge.

Every day is a new day with Cupid. He loves the water and has weekly therapy swimming lessons to strengthen his back legs. He requires a lifejacket to keep his head above the water, but that never slows him down! To help with his disability, Cupid has been fitted for front leg prosthetics and skis and now a wheelchair. He's seventy pounds and cruises around with his wheelchair, which gives him the ability to run, to stand still, to sit, to spin around,

and most importantly to sniff the ground. No dog loves his daily walks and other furry family members more than Cupid.

I work in the animal health field, and one day I went to do a presentation at a local humane society. Just the day before a puppy had come into the shelter and was barking up a storm. One of the receptionists brought Ginger out of her cage, and she was so nervous and afraid. I saw her and started oohing and aahing over her, and then I held her on my lap during my entire presentation. That's all it took. The deal was done! I took a selfie with Ginger and sent it to my husband, and I went home with my precious bundle.

Ginger fit in perfectly with our family. She is the cutest/oddest mixed

breed dog! People always ask, "What breed is she?" I tell them that she is happily my forever "purebred Brown dog." We just love her to pieces!

A Word from Cupid and Ginger

Determine what you want, and bark loud. Persevere. One wag may not always do the job.

It started with a random search for a family dog on a humane society Facebook page, when my wife found Hector, a purebred blue Weimaraner. Can you imagine that a seventy-pound, highly energetic sport dog had been meant to be a companion dog of a sixty-year-old widow? No wonder Hector found his way into the humane society.

Our intent was just to make a casual visit to look at him, but the sight of his incredible coat shimmering in the afternoon sunlight was too much. The kids begged me to run and get him to chase me, and it worked. It was a weird instant bond…almost like I had with some of our family dogs growing up. We talked about adopting Hector, but then we learned that one family had visited with Hector every day that week. Later, when I called our adoption assistant and told her we thought perhaps the other family needed Hector more than we did, she was quickly disappointed and said that based on our interaction with him and our family's outdoor lifestyle, they felt we were an ideal fit and asked us to please reconsider.

I have no idea why, but as soon as I clicked off the phone, I got very emotional and began to weep. I could hardly explain it to my wife,

which is totally out of character for me.
I was a sobbing mess. When we told
the kids we were adopting Hector, they
went nuts, hugs and kisses all around,
including the dog, big slobber kisses. It
was done. Hector was ours!

So you ask, what about Duke? Well,
Hector just didn't seem like the right name for a dog in a family
of Irish ancestry. So Hector became Duke, and within twelve hours
Duke had a forever home and we have a forever Duke.

As for Duke, he is awesome and has enriched our lives beyond
words. He fills our hearts with happiness every day. Hiking and biking
and more, Duke is always there making us laugh and loving us. Duke
gives the kids such joy. He's not allowed on any furniture except on
the kids' beds at night, and oh how he
loves to snuggle right up as if he is an
extension of their bodies!

As for me, Duke still gives me that
amazing feeling. When I come home
and he greets me at the door, and I see

his smiling face, his ears tucked back and out, and hear his voice, it hits me in the heart every time. When I'm depressed, I cuddle with Duke. When I'm frustrated, I walk with Duke. When I'm bored, I wrestle with Duke. I even take a few minutes every day and hug Duke just as my kids do.

Our lives are forever changed. Duke completes our family, and I can't imagine our lives without him.

A Word from Duke

Celebrate when your loved ones come home.
Live with gusto, passion, and pleasure.
Never waste a good bone!

Dog breeds come in all shapes and sizes and throughout history have been bred to perform a wide range of tasks. What do you get when you mix many breeds, including Akita, Labrador, Bullmastiff, and Havanese, into one dog? You get our somewhat quirky rescue dog, Scout.

Scout was left in a box with five littermates outside a local humane society. Our family was checking on the society's adoption page from time to time, hoping to find just the right dog, and when we saw her in the middle of the litter, we knew it was time to move. We went in and were delighted to find that she was the last puppy left. We adopted her on the spot.

Someone at the humane society had given her the name Margo. That didn't work for us. Our son had recently read *To Kill a Mockingbird*, and he was passionate to name her Scout. Our daughter, who was eight at the time, countered that she be named Princess Buttercup. So we spent time in family negotiations and finally agreed that Buttercup would be her middle name. Scout Buttercup…trust me, it grows on you over time.

We hoped that Scout would force us to be more active, but she is a naturally lazy dog. The more cultured might say she is easygoing or laidback or even understated. She loves to go for car rides, especially dance carpool, but when she sees her leash coming out, she literally hides in the corner of the dining room. Get the picture? What could be better than to lie sprawled out on the carpet or to sit back and watch the world go by? Why sprint when you can stroll? To show your interest, raise your head slightly and give a wag of the tail. That's the life!

A Word from Scout

Don't take life or yourself too seriously. Leave room in your schedule for naps-lots of naps. Enjoy the moment! Go for a joyride!

Not surprisingly, Scout is a quiet dog that also loves to eat. Mealtimes may be the only times when you see her move quickly. How much does she love to eat? Truth to tell, she will often stand in front of her bowl and insist that she hasn't been fed yet…after she has already eaten! Sir Walter Scott said, "Recollect that the Almighty, who gave the dog to be companion of our pleasures and our toils, hath invested him with a nature noble and incapable of deceit." He obviously never saw Scout gazing up with her eager, innocent eyes, pleading for her bowl to be filled, with food crumbs still fresh on her lower lip. So many Oscar-worthy performances from Scout make us laugh and laugh.

Of course, her favorite food is…pizza.

As you can tell, Scout is a beloved family member, a bit out of shape, but a wonderful and comfortable companion.